Islands

by Kimberly M. Hutmacher

Consulting Editor: Gail Saunders-Smith, PhD

Consultant: Nikki Strong, PhD
St. Anthony Falls Laboratory
University of Minnesota

CAPSTONE PRESS
a capstone imprint

Pebble Plus is published by Capstone Press,
151 Good Counsel Drive, P.O. Box 669, Mankato, Minnesota 56002.
www.capstonepub.com

Books published by Capstone Press are manufactured with paper
containing at least 10 percent post-consumer waste.

Library of Congress Cataloging-in-Publication Data
Hutmacher, Kimberly.
  Islands / by Kimberly M. Hutmacher.
    p. cm. — (Pebble plus, natural wonders)
  Includes bibliographical references and index.
  Summary: "Simple text and color photographs explain how islands form, types of islands, and life on islands"—
Provided by publisher.
  ISBN 978-1-4296-5321-3 (library binding)
  ISBN 978-1-4296-6219-2 (paperback)
  1. Islands—Juvenile literature. 2. Islands. I. Title. II. Series.
  GB471.H88 2011
  551.42—dc22   2010029079

Editorial Credits
Gillia Olson, editor; Heidi Thompson, designer; Eric Manske, production specialist

Photo Credits
Alamy/FLPA, 7; Photoshot Holdings Ltd, 13; Russ Bishop, 15
Dreamstime/Gregsi, cover; Intrepix, 20
Getty Images Inc./Photolibrary/Robin Bush, 17; Visuals Unlimited/Ashley Cooper, 21; Dr. Frank Hanna, 11
NASA/GSFC/Jacques Descloitres, MODIS Rapid Response Team, 18
Peter Arnold/Biosphoto/Cordier Sylvain, 5
Shutterstock/BrendanReals, 19; Gina Sanders, 9; Marrero Imagery, 1

Note to Parents and Teachers

The Natural Wonders series supports national geography standards related to the physical and
human characteristics of places. This book describes and illustrates islands. The images support
early readers in understanding the text. The repetition of words and phrases helps early readers
learn new words. This book also introduces early readers to subject-specific vocabulary words,
which are defined in the Glossary section. Early readers may need assistance to read some
words and to use the Table of Contents, Glossary, Read More, Internet Sites, and Index sections
of the book.

Printed in the United States of America in North Mankato, Minnesota.
092010   005933CGS11

Table of Contents

An Island Forms

Long ago, the sea level rose.

Water filled low spots on land.

Pieces of land were separated

from the mainland by water.

Continental islands were born.

Kinds of Islands

Continental islands were part of continents. But oceanic islands form in the middle of the ocean. Underwater volcanoes pile up lava on the ocean floor.

Coral reefs form coral islands.
Sometimes the sea level drops or
land under the reef rises.
Coral that breaks the water's
surface forms an island.

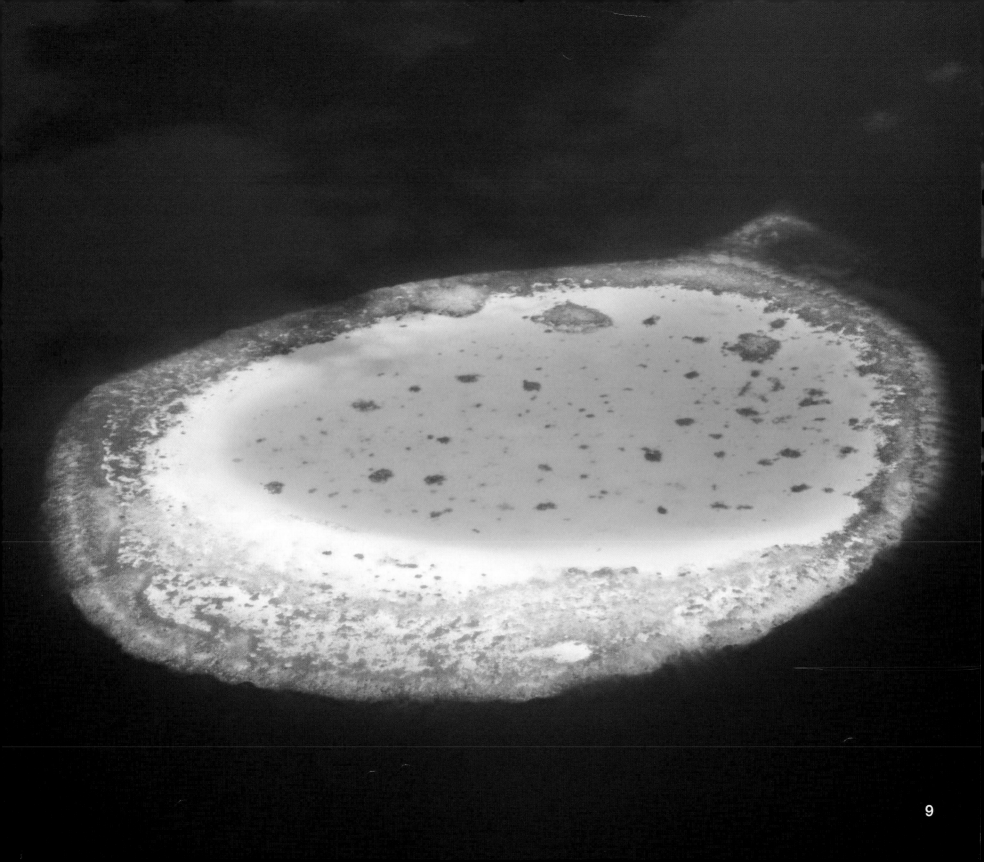

Barrier islands form near

the shores of continents.

Wind and water pile up sand

from the ocean floor.

Island Life

Life on continental islands

is often like the mainland.

Similar plants and animals

lived there when water cut off

the mainland.

Volcanic islands start with no life.

Birds and insects fly there.

Wind and water bring

plant seeds. Coconut trees

got to Hawaii this way.

Isolated oceanic islands
often have animals unlike
any mainland animals.
The kiwi bird is found only
on the island of New Zealand.

Famous Islands

Islands often form in chains.

The Hawaiian Islands

include eight big islands.

The chain also has many

small islands called islets.

Hawaiian
Islands

Greenland is the largest

island in the world.

It covers 840,000 square miles

(2,175,600 square kilometers).

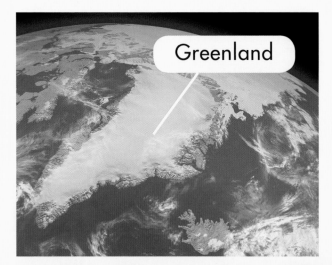

Greenland

Glossary

continent—one of the seven main landmasses of Earth; they are Africa, Antarctica, Asia, Australia, Europe, North America and South America

coral—an ocean animal with a soft body and many tentacles; corals often live in groups; coral reefs are made from the hardened skeletons of corals

islet—a very small island

isolated—cut off or separated from something

lava—hot rock that pours out of a volcano

mainland—the largest piece of a continent, as opposed to its islands

sea level—the average level of the surface of the ocean

volcano—a crack in the Earth's surface formed when hot rock inside the Earth is forced out

Read More

Mayer, Cassie. *Islands*. Landforms. Heinemann Library, 2007.

Salas, Laura Purdie. *Coral Reefs: Colorful Underwater Habitats*. Amazing Science: Ecosystems. Minneapolis: Picture Window Books, 2009.

Schaefer, Lola M. *An Island Grows*. New York: Greenwillow Books, 2006.

Internet Sites

FactHound offers a safe, fun way to find Internet sites related to this book. All of the sites on FactHound have been researched by our staff.

Here's all you do:

Visit *www.facthound.com*

Type in this code: 9781429653213

Super-cool stuff! Check out projects, games and lots more at **www.capstonekids.com**

Index

Word Count: 198
Grade: 1
Early-Intervention Level: 20